JAN 17 2013

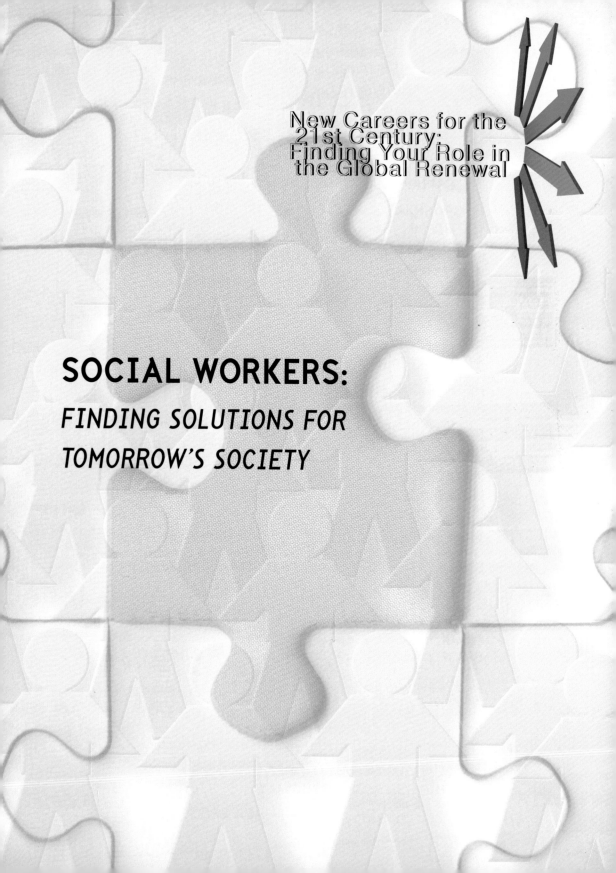

New Careers for the 21st Century: Finding Your Role in the Global Renewal

SOCIAL WORKERS:

FINDING SOLUTIONS FOR TOMORROW'S SOCIETY

New Careers for the 21st Century: Finding Your Role in the Global Renewal

New Careers for the
21st Century:
Finding Your Role in
the Global Renewal

SOCIAL WORKERS:

FINDING SOLUTIONS FOR
TOMORROW'S SOCIETY

by Camden Flath

Mason Crest Publishers

SOCIAL WORKERS:

FINDING SOLUTIONS FOR TOMORROW'S SOCIETY

MASON CREST PUBLISHERS INC.
370 Reed Road
Broomall, Pennsylvania 19008
(866)MCP-BOOK (toll free)
www.masoncrest.com

First Printing
9 8 7 6 5 4 3 2 1

Library of Congress Cataloging-in-Publication Data

Flath, Camden, 1987-
   Social workers : finding solutions for tomorrow's society / by Camden Flath.
       p. cm.
   Includes bibliographical references and index.
   ISBN 978-1-4222-1821-1   ISBN 978-1-4222-1811-2 (series)
   ISBN 978-1-4222-2042-9 (ppb)   ISBN 978-1-4222-2032-0 (series ppb)
   1. Social service—Vocational guidance—Juvenile literature. 2. Social workers—Juvenile literature. I. Title.
   HV10.5.F63 2011
   361.3023—dc22
                                   2010017920

Produced by Harding House Publishing Service, Inc.
www.hardinghousepages.com
Interior Design by MK Bassett-Harvey.
Cover design by Torque Advertising + Design.
Printed in USA by Bang Printing.

CONTENTS

INTRODUCTION

Be careful as you begin to plan your career.

To get yourself in the best position to begin the career of your dreams, you need to know what the "green world" will look like and what jobs will be created and what jobs will become obsolete. Just think, according to the Bureau of Labor Statistics, the following jobs are expected to severely decline by 2012:

- word processors and data-entry keyers

- stock clerks and order fillers

- secretaries

- electrical and electronic equipment assemblers

- computer operators

- telephone operators

- postal service mail sorters and processing-machine operators

- travel agents

These are just a few of the positions that will decrease or become obsolete as we move forward into the century.

You need to know what the future jobs will be. How do you find them? One way is to look where money is being invested. Many firms and corporations are now making investments in startup and research enterprises. These companies may become the "Microsoft" and "Apple" of the twenty-first century. Look at what is being researched and what technology is needed to obtain the results.

Green world, green economy, green technology—they all say the same things: the way we do business today is changing. Every industry will be shaped by the world's new focus on creating a sustainable lifestyle, one that won't deplete our natural and economic resources.

The possibilities are unlimited. Almost any area that will conserve energy and reduce the dependency on fossil fuels is open to new and exciting career paths. Many of these positions have not even been identified yet and will only come to light as the technology progresses and new discoveries are made in the way we use that technology. And the best part about this is that our government is behind us. The U.S. government wants to help you get the education and training you'll need to succeed and grow in this new and changing economy. The U.S. Department of Labor has launched a series of initiatives to support and promote green job creation. To view the report, visit: www.dol.gov/dol/green/earthday_reportA.pdf.

The time to decide on your future is now. This series, NEW CAREERS FOR THE 21ST CENTURY: FINDING YOUR ROLE IN THE GLOBAL RENEWAL, can act as the first step toward your continued education, training, and career path decisions. Take the first steps that will lead you—and the planet—to a productive and sustainable future.

Mike Puglisi
Department of Labor, District I Director (New York/New Jersey)
IAWP (International Association of Workforce Professionals)

An entirely new system of thought is needed, a system based on attention to people, and not primarily attention to goods.

—E. F. Schumacher

ABOUT THE QUOTE

Our world is changing—and people are starting to understand that many of the important answers to the world's problems lie in finding solutions for individuals who are caught in circumstances beyond their control. Social workers don't create a product. They don't sell anything. They don't make or build anything. Instead, they pay attention to people, empowering them to find ways to rise above their circumstances.

CHAPTER 1
WHAT IS SOCIAL WORK?

WORDS TO KNOW

welfare: Financial help, and help providing food and housing, given by the government to those in need.

policy: The course of action decided on by an organization or government body.

advocating: Arguing and working for something.

foster care: Care in private or group homes for children whose parents are unable or unwilling to provide for them.

terminal: Involving or causing the end of life; leading to death.

chronic: Continuing for a long time.

private practice: Working independently rather than for an agency.

halfway houses: Residences for people who have been released from an institution, such as a prison, hospital, or rehabilitation program, and are transitioning to life in the outside world.

group homes: Residences for people needing care of some sort—such as foster children or those with physical or mental challenges.

As technology advances, the world becomes more interconnected, and more people have greater access to more information than ever before, our society must still cope with old problems. Problems like crushing poverty, deadly diseases, drug addiction, and violence have been a part of daily life for many in the United States and around the world for centuries, and they continue to be a challenge to our society today.

As the divide between the earnings of the poorest and richest Americans widens each year, as children go without adequate nutrition because their parents cannot provide it for them, as sick senior citizens suffer illness without proper medical care, the need is growing for people who are willing to help individuals with these issues. Today, the demand is high and predicted to continue to increase for workers committed to a career in serving people who need assistance.

Today's young adults will become the workers and job seekers of the future. For young people entering the workforce in the early twenty-first century, seeking a career in line with the world's changing needs can be a great way to find fulfilling and productive work.

Over the next decade, some occupations are projected to grow more than others. The number of people employed in careers related to social work, for instance, is expected to grow faster than employment in many other job industries. The United States Department of Labor's Bureau of Labor Statistics projects that while the average rate of growth for jobs across all industries is

11 percent through 2018, jobs in social work are on track to grow around 16 percent in the same period of time.

SOCIAL WORKERS

Social work is an occupation devoted to helping make people's lives better in a variety of ways. Social workers help people solve problems ranging from family, professional, or personal difficulties. Social workers may help clients with disabilities, those who have a disease, or individuals with issues that include poor housing, lack of employment opportunities, or drug abuse. Social workers may also help families dealing with domestic abuse of a child or spouse.

Cole Weeks is a Family Advocacy social worker. He works with families to prevent or treat abuse.

Social workers may be needed to help in disaster situations. These social workers are waiting to assist U.S. citizens evacuated from Haiti in the wake of the earthquake that hit the country in February 2010.

Social workers also sometimes help individuals who qualify for social services (services provided by the state to those in need) to access government assistance. This may include financial help from social *welfare* programs, programs that allow people to buy food, pay for medical care, and provide for their families. Social workers might help someone with a drug addiction seek treatment, counseling, or care at a rehabilitation center.

Some social workers are employed to carry out research on specific *policy* issues. These workers may be involved in *advocating* for better social services by organizing citizen groups or collecting information on a particular issue.

Social workers who hold a license from the state in which they work may be called licensed clinical social workers. Many social workers choose to specialize in a specific area of their field, perhaps focusing on one population, social problem, or environment. Three main categories of social workers cover the majority of workers in the field. Each of these categories includes a diverse range of positions, roles, and responsibilities.

CHILD, FAMILY, AND SCHOOL SOCIAL WORKERS

Child, family, and school social workers focus on helping improve the lives of children and their parents by providing them with social services. These social workers look at the needs of a family and coordinate the services that would be of assistance; they may work with a single parent to find her child day care, for instance. Child, family, and school social workers may also set up adoptions, working with *foster care* programs, children, and parents. Some social workers place children in foster homes after they are abused or abandoned. A child, family, or school social worker might choose to specialize in a particular social issue (such as child abuse or foster care) or work exclusively in a specific setting.

School social workers communicate with students and their parents, teachers, and school administrators about how to make sure young people are reaching their potential in the classroom and personally. Students who are having emotional problems may work with a school social worker to get assistance. Children with disabilities and their parents can also speak with a school social worker in order to work with the school or find assistance in the larger community.

Child, family, and school social workers are sometimes also called child welfare social workers, child protective services social workers, or family services social workers. They are employed in schools, at family services agencies, and by the government.

MEDICAL AND PUBLIC HEALTH SOCIAL WORKERS

Medical and public health social workers give support to people who have *terminal* or *chronic* illness. These ailments include Alzheimer's disease, cancer, AIDS, and HIV. These social workers also help the families of individuals with illness understand the needs of the patients, as well as how to give them the care they need when they are at home. These social workers may make plans for a client to receive in-home services like having food delivered or home care from a medical professional.

Some medical and public health social workers specialize in caring for senior citizens. They may plan long-term care, transportation, and housing for elderly clients. These workers may also coordinate support for the families of the aging, including possibly running group counseling meetings. Social workers who specialize in elderly care and services for senior citizens are known as gerontological social workers.

Medical and public health social workers are employed in hospitals, private care facilities, or family service agencies. Local governments employ many of these social workers, as well.

Mental Health and Substance Abuse Social Workers

Mental health and substance abuse social workers examine the needs of individuals with mental illness or substance abuse issues and work to get them treatment. They may have clients attend therapy or go to a rehabilitation program. In addition, when clients leave rehabilitation or a live-in care facility, mental health and substance abuse social workers make sure the clients can continue to receive any treatment they need. These social workers may also help families cope with the hardships of drug and alcohol abuse or mental illness.

Mental health and substance abuse social workers may be employed at outpatient facilities, places where clients come for treatment but live elsewhere, or in-patient facilities, where patients live at the facility. Some may work for employee assistance organizations, helping people find work while they are recovering from mental health issues or if they have histories of drug abuse. Others work in *private practices* and can be called clinical social workers.

OTHER SOCIAL WORKERS

Other social workers work as researchers, policymakers, or social work administrators. These social workers focus their efforts on examining social problems and offering solutions to the issues of poverty, violence, homelessness, and drug abuse. They may work

Did You Know?
By 2018, the Bureau of Labor Statistics projects that 103,400 more people will be employed as social workers than in 2008.

Some social workers specialize in working with children in schools. These workers make sure children are reaching their potential, and determine if there are any problems that need to be addressed.

with legislators, raise money for causes, or analyze the function of social programs and policies.

SOCIAL AND HUMAN SERVICE ASSISTANTS

Social and human service assistants aid social workers, healthcare professionals, and individuals in related positions to provide services to individuals. "Social and human service assistants" is a broad term used to describe workers in a variety of positions, including:

- human service worker

- case management aide

- social work assistant

- mental health aide

- community outreach worker

- social services aide

- life skills counselor

- youth worker

Often, social and human service assistants work under professionals in psychiatry, psychology, nursing, or social work. Depending on the field in which they work, as well as the position they hold, workers in social and human service assistance will have differing responsibilities and levels of supervision. Some social service assistants may run programs or facilities, while others are required to work closely with a supervisor.

Social and human service assistants, like social workers, provide services to individual clients in order to better their lives. They must learn about what a client needs, look into whether the client is eligible to receive social services (such as food stamps, welfare, or Medicaid), and then work with the client to get them the services for which they qualify. Social and human services assistants may help clients with transportation (to meetings with a doctor or lawyer, for instance) or provide encouragement and positive support. These workers keep records of each client's case, reporting changes or progress to their supervisors or the social worker acting as case manager.

Workers employed as social and human service assistants work to help their communities in many ways. These workers may

A food bank is an organization that collects and distributes food to individuals, or to agencies who then distribute food to the hungry.

run food banks or help individuals in times of crisis. They may work in *halfway houses* or *group homes*, helping adults who need help with everyday tasks like hygiene. Social and human service assistants may be responsible for making sure that client records are kept correctly. They may speak with the families of clients as well as medical professionals. In many cases, assistants help their clients' caregivers understand the needs of their loved ones. In hospitals and rehabilitation clinics, social and human service assistants work alongside medical, psychiatric, and social work professionals to assist their clients with treatment, daily tasks, and communicating with others. They may help their clients maintain their plan of treatment by attending counseling or therapy with them.

Working as a social or human service assistant can be fulfilling, but it can also be very demanding. Often, social service programs are understaffed, meaning that assistants may be responsible for more work or have to work long hours. In addition, social and human service assistants often aren't paid as well as workers in other occupations.

CAREERS IN SOCIAL WORK: CHILD, FAMILY, AND SCHOOL SOCIAL WORKERS

Child, family, and school social workers have a variety of responsibilities including:

• speaking with individuals and their families about mental health issues, poverty, drug abuse, violence, child care, and medical treatment, among other subjects.

- examining carefully the needs of an individual client through interviews with the client and his family.

- deciding which services can best help children and their families with a particular problem (such as drug abuse, violence, or disease).

- keeping detailed case records for each client with whom they work, as well as creating reports on cases to present to their supervisors.

- discussing legal issues with children and their parents. This might include providing testimony in court or helping a child prepare for a hearing.

- speaking with parents about the cause of their child's misbehavior or law breaking, and offering potential solutions to these root problems.

- recommending organizations within a community that can help clients or their families get help with a wide range of problems, including unemployment, financial counseling, legal assistance, and medical care, among others.

- coordinating students, families, schools, and social services organizations to help kids who face issues of poverty, disability, or violence.

Child, family, and school social workers must also carry out tasks not always directly related to their field. Gathering information and research on a specific topic, for instance, is something that social workers in all fields must do on a regular basis. Child, family, and school social workers must communicate with the people with whom they work, including supervisors and coworkers, as to what they are working on and the progress they are making. Workers may need to communicate with people outside their own organization to coordinate services for their clients. They must decide, based on the information they can gather about clients through speaking with them and their families, which services can best improve their clients' lives. Decision-making skills are often the core strengths for social workers who work with children, their families, and schools. In addition, some social workers in this field may be called upon to interact with the public, discussing a specific issue at a group meeting or through different types of media.

Skills and Experience

Child, family, and school social workers must have the necessary knowledge to perform their duties effectively. These workers must understand the basics of therapy and counseling, for instance, in order to coordinate care, treatment, and assistance for children with mental or physical health problems. Social workers who are working with children with behavioral problems must understand human behavior and psychology in order to decide how best to help a child, school, or family. They must understand how children behave in groups and among friends, as well as how to work with kids from different cultural backgrounds. Child, family, and school social workers must also know about legal issues

What Kind of Person Are You?

Career-counseling experts know that certain kinds of people do best in certain kinds of jobs. John L. Holland developed the following list of personality types and the kinds of jobs that are the best match for each type. See which one (or two) are most like you. The more you understand yourself, the better you'll be able to make a good career plan for yourself.

- **Realistic personality:** This kind of person likes to do practical, hands-on work. He or she will most enjoy working with materials that can be touched and manipulated, such as wood, steel, tools, and machinery. This personality type enjoys jobs that require working outdoors, but he or she does NOT enjoy jobs that require a lot of paperwork or close teamwork with others.

- **Investigative personality**: This personality type likes to work with ideas. He or she will enjoy jobs that require lots of thinking and researching. Jobs that require mental problem solving will be a good fit for this personality.

- **Artistic personality:** This type of person enjoys working with forms, designs, and patterns. She or he likes jobs that require self-expression—and that don't require following a definite set of rules.

- **Social personality:** Jobs that require lots of teamwork with others, as well as teaching others, are a good match for this personality type. These jobs often involve helping others in some way.

- **Enterprising personality:** This person will enjoy planning and starting new projects, even if that involves a degree of risk-taking. He or she is good at making decisions and leading others.

- **Conventional personality:** An individual with this type of personality likes to follow a clear set of procedures or routines. He or she doesn't want to be the boss but prefers to work under someone else's leadership. Jobs that require working with details and facts (more than ideas) are a good fit for this personality.

surrounding their work. Knowledge of laws, legal procedures, and government regulations, for example, can be of great help to these workers.

Did You Know?

By 2018, the Bureau of Labor Statistics expects employment in child, family, and school social work to grow at a rate of 12 percent.

In addition to a basis of knowledge in their field, child, family, and school social workers must have excellent written and verbal communication skills. It is vitally important that these social workers understand how to talk with kids, medical professionals, school administrators, parents, lawyers, and anyone else involved in the care of the children they are working to help. They also must have a good understanding of current methods of communication, including the use of computers for record keeping, e-mail communication with clients' families, and managing digital files.

All the world is full of suffering. It is also full of overcoming it.

—Helen Keller

ABOUT THE QUOTE

Social workers must be able to look directly at the world's suffering—and then find positive, constructive ways to overcome that suffering.

CHAPTER 2
EDUCATION AND TRAINING

Words to Know

bachelor's degree: The degree received after completing a specific course of study at a college or university, usually taking four years.

master's degree: A higher level degree for those who have already earned a bachelor's degree, usually taking one to two years to complete.

social justice: The idea of bringing justice to society and involving things such as human rights and equality.

fieldwork: Work done in the field—in the "real world"—as opposed to in a classroom or office.

sociology: The study of human society and how it develops and functions.

public sector: Agencies and organizations run by the government, as opposed to privately.

associate's degree: A degree received at a college or community college, open to those with a high school diploma, usually taking two years to complete.

liberal arts: Courses providing general knowledge in arts, humanities, and sciences, rather than in technical or career-specific fields.

legal precedents: Decisions made in court cases that set up the outcomes of similar cases in the future.

T he majority of positions in social services require that job applicants have at least a *bachelor's degree* and many require a *master's degree*, but entry-level social and human services assistant jobs may only require a high school education. Many higher-level social work careers, in management or supervising, for instance, require advanced degrees in social work or social sciences. The further a person takes her education, the more qualified she will be for jobs in social services.

SOCIAL WORKERS

BACHELOR'S DEGREE

A bachelor's degree is a requirement for those entering a career in social work, though many positions require that job applicants hold an advanced degree. Every state in the country, as well as Washington D.C., requires that those who wish to become social workers become licensed, certified, or registered, but the way that social workers are regulated can be different from state to state.

Bachelor's degree coursework often includes social work ethics, *social justice*, cultural diversity, human behavior, and welfare policy, among other subjects. These degree programs prepare students for positions as caseworkers, mental health assistants, and residential facility counselors. Many bachelor's degree programs require that students complete 400 hours of *fieldwork* under supervision.

A bachelor's degree in social work, known as a BSW, is the minimum requirement for a majority of social worker positions.

Some smaller social service agencies may hire workers who have degrees in psychology or *sociology* for entry-level positions.

Graduate Degrees

While a bachelor's degree is enough to enter social work, workers with advanced degrees will be qualified for more jobs. To be considered for a job in medical or school social work, for instance, applicants will usually need to have a master's degree in social work (MSW). In some cases, employers may seek social workers who have an MSW with a concentration in a specific area, such as social policy. Work as a supervisor or administrator of a social

An education in social work will include a variety of courses, from nursing to law.

services agency will also require an advanced degree. Beyond a MSW, social workers can go on to get a doctorate in social work (DSW). This kind of degree is required for university-level teaching positions, as well as some positions in social research.

Though a bachelor's degree in social work is not always necessary when entering a master's degree program in social work, many programs look highly upon students who hold a BSW when considering applicants. MSW programs often involve at least 900 hours of supervised work experience, internship, or field education. Students complete program requirements over the course of two years for full-time students and up to four years for part-time students. Graduates of master's degree programs learn to manage many cases at once, supervise others, and meet client needs in new ways.

Did You Know?
In the United States, 468 bachelor's-level and 196 master's-level social work programs (BSW and MSW, respectively) were accredited by the Council on Social Work Education (CSWE) as of 2009.

LICENSURE

All states and the District of Columbia require that social workers become licensed or registered in some way. This means that in order to practice as a social worker, individuals must comply with the state's rules and requirements, completing a set amount of supervised work experience, or a two-year program. Each state has different requirements for social workers applying for their license. Unlicensed social workers may not work in a majority of social work positions, though those hoping to become licensed may work as social services assistants. Each state also decides the settings in which unlicensed social workers can work.

OTHER QUALIFICATIONS

Social workers must be able to deal with what are often troubling subjects and sensitive situations. This means they must exhibit responsibility, understanding, and emotional maturity, particularly when working with clients. Social workers often work independently, but they also must maintain good relationships with their coworkers. For those who hope to become social workers, working as social service assistants can be a good way to get experience with the kind of work they might do in the future.

ADVANCEMENT

Social workers who seek to advance their careers will usually need a master's degree and work experience. Social workers may move up to supervise others, manage social service programs, or direct a social service agency. They may choose to go into teaching, policy advocacy, or private consulting. Some social workers go on to work with legislators in crafting policy or analyzing the effects of government social policy at a research institution.

Some social workers leave the *public sector* and move to working for private practices, or they might begin private practices of their own. Private social workers are clinical social workers who are paid by their clients directly, or paid through the health insurance companies covering their clients. Social workers employed by private practices have a master's degree (at the minimum) and on-the-job experience. These social workers must be able to maintain good relationships with clients, as well as with coworkers and other social workers (who may refer clients to private practices).

SOCIAL AND HUMAN SERVICE ASSISTANTS

EDUCATION AND TRAINING

Though graduation from high school is often the only kind of formal education required by employers hiring social or human service assistants, workers who have additional education or work

Social service assistants with only a high school degree may help clients fill out complicated paperwork.

experience will be more likely to find employment than those job seekers who do not. *Associate degrees* in human services or in one of the social sciences will also help workers to qualify for positions as social or human service assistants. Some employers may look specifically for workers with bachelor's or master's degrees in human services, counseling, or social work.

Human services degree coursework usually includes training in observing patients, record keeping, conducting patient interviews, and case management processes. Human services programs often have students working in the field, gaining work experience as they further their education. In addition to degree-related courses, students in these programs will often also take *liberal arts* and science classes. Students may be required to complete an internship in some degree programs.

A worker's level of education often determines the sort of work he is assigned when starting his career in social or human services. Workers with only a high school education may help clients fill out paperwork in a social service agency, for instance, while college graduates may be able to start out their careers in counseling, program planning, or residential facility management. Employers often train new employees in the tasks they will be performing, either on the job or in seminars and workshops.

OTHER QUALIFICATIONS

In order to work effectively as a social or human service assistant, workers must have solid communication and time-management skills. Workers in this occupation must have a desire to help people, be understanding of others, and show patience with what can be frustrating work. Employers today often check the criminal background of potential social or human service assistants. Some employers may require that workers have a driver's license and car.

ADVANCEMENT

Most social and health service assistants will need a college degree to advance in their career paths. Generally, promotion to positions in case management and social work will require a bachelor's degree or master's degree in counseling, human services, social work, or similar fields.

CAREERS IN SOCIAL WORK: MENTAL HEALTH AND SUBSTANCE ABUSE SOCIAL WORKERS

Mental health and substance abuse social workers must:

- speak with people in one-on-one and group settings about drug and alcohol abuse, mental illness, and the effect that poverty, unemployment, and physical health can have on these individuals.

- assess the individual needs of clients by speaking with them and their families, looking over their records, and speaking with other professional social workers as well as medical professionals if needed.

- work with others (including medical personnel and counselors) to plan treatment around the needs of patients with mental health or substance abuse issues.

- keep track of clients' treatment goals, evaluating progress and informing supervisors of case developments.

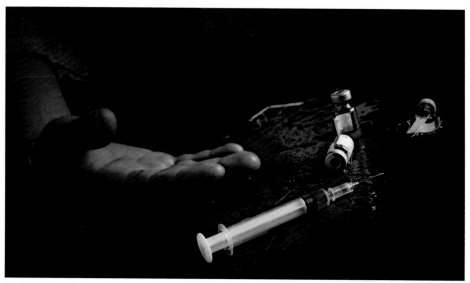

Substance abuse plays a role in many major social problems, such as drugged driving, violence, stress and child abuse. Drug abuse can lead to homelessness, crime, and missed work or problems with keeping a job.

- work with the community to inform people of issues in mental health, abuse of drugs and alcohol, and treatment for these problems, including pointing people to community resources.

- help clients stay on their treatment plans. This might mean that social workers set up appointments for clients and arrange for transportation to and from appointments.

- recommend community resources that might help clients find housing or treatment for a mental illness. Social workers must make sure their clients follow through on their recommendations.

- observe changes in the status and needs of client, and make changes in treatment plans.

- speak with family members of clients with mental illnesses or drug abuse problems, providing them with support in dealing with their loved one.

Mental health and substance abuse social workers must also make sure they are up to date on the latest information in their field. This might mean reading social research or conducting studies themselves;

Did You Know?
By 2018, the Bureau of Labor Statistics expects the rate of growth in employment among mental health and substance abuse social workers to grow by 20 percent.

reading literature on social issues and potential solutions; and going to classes or seminars focusing on social issues such as drug abuse and mental illness. Workers should consistently strive to apply the latest knowledge to their daily work in order to best serve the clients with whom they work.

SKILLS AND EXPERIENCE

Mental health and substance abuse social workers must have extensive knowledge of subjects not directly related to their work. Like other social workers, mental health and substance abuse social workers must understand the different laws that may affect their clients. An understanding of court procedures, social service agency regulations, and *legal precedents* will be very helpful for these social workers. Mental health and substance abuse social workers must also have knowledge of therapy and counseling techniques and procedures, so that they can effectively recommend resources and care to their clients. In addition, knowledge of psychology can help these social workers understand their clients better, allowing them to more accurately assess their needs. Keeping up on trends in job preparedness and education can also help social workers recommend services to clients re-entering daily life after receiving treatment for mental illness or drug addiction.

In some cases, mental health and substance abuse social workers will need to employ knowledge of different cultural attitudes toward mental illness and drug use. Understanding how a client's culture affects their ability to get treatment or support can be vitally important to a social worker.

If You Have a Social Personality . . .

Social work is an ideal field for you to pursue. Social work positions, as well as assistant positions, will give you many opportunities to help people who need you. Since you're genuinely and warmly interested in people and their problems, these careers will keep you constantly interested in your work life—and that's a good thing! You probably don't enjoy using machines and tools, and they're not likely to be a part of a social worker's professional life.

If You Have a Conventional Personality . . .

You might like being an assistant in this field, where your ability to follow directions in an orderly way will be an asset to you.

Your imagination is your preview of life's coming attractions.

—Albert Einstein

CHAPTER 3
JOB OPPORTUNITIES

Words to Know

residential facility: A treatment center in which patients live at the center while they are being treated.

physical therapy: The care and treatment of pain or disability using massage and exercise rather than medicines and surgery.

Social services jobs (including both social workers and social and human services assistants) take place in a variety of settings. As varied as the demand for social services are, so too are the environments in which social workers assist their clients. Whether in a hospital, group home, or rehabilitation clinic, social workers and assistants are helping people get the services they need. Though the work may be stressful or emotionally overwhelming at times, the rewards in helping others can give workers in social services a fulfilling, if demanding, career.

SOCIAL WORKERS

WORK ENVIRONMENT

Social workers typically spend the majority of their time working in an office or *residential facility*. Some cases may require that social workers travel to meet clients, though often social workers will only have to travel in their area. Some organizations or social service programs have multiple offices, requiring social workers to meet with clients at one of many offices. Many social workers work a standard forty-hour week, but some work nights or weekends if certain clients or particular cases require it. Attending community meetings, often held at night or on weekends, may also be required of social workers. Some social workers work part time or volunteer their time and skills to nonprofit social agencies.

Social work, while often quite satisfying, can be extraordinarily demanding. In most places, demand for social services is high, while social service agencies are understaffed. This means that fewer social workers see more clients and must manage more cases. Those seeking work in social services should be aware of the demands of the occupation.

EMPLOYMENT

According to the Bureau of Labor Statistics, social workers held around 642,000 jobs in 2008. Of these workers, 54 percent were employed in the healthcare and social assistance industries. Thirty-one percent were employed by government agencies,

Employment by Type of Social Worker, 2008	
Child, family, and school social workers	292,600
Medical and public health social workers	138,700
Mental health and substance abuse workers	137,300
Social workers, all other	73,400

This table shows the distribution of social workers by job type for 2008. The majority of these positions require at least a bachelor's degree in social work.

at either the state or local level. The majority of social workers worked in cities or suburbs, as opposed to rural areas, where fewer social workers are employed.

In 2008, 292,600 child, family, and school social workers; 138,700 medical and public health social workers; and 137,700 mental health and substance abuse social workers were employed in their particular fields, while 73,400 social workers were working in all other fields of social work.

EARNINGS

The average yearly income of child, family, and school social workers was just under $40,000 in 2008. The highest-earning 10 percent of these workers earned an average of more than $66,000 per year. The lowest-earning 10 percent made around $25,000 yearly, on average. The middle 50 percent of child, family, and social workers made between $31,000 and $52,000 annually.

In May 2008, the average yearly wages in the industries employing the most child, family, and school social workers were:

Elementary and secondary schools	$53,860
Local government	46,650
State government	39,600
Individual and family services	34,450
Other residential care facilities	34,270

[From http://www.bls.gov/oco/ocos060.htm]

In 2008, the Bureau of Labor Statistics (BLS) reported that medical and public health social workers made an average yearly income of approximately $46,600. On average, the highest-paid 10 percent of workers in this occupation made around $69,000 per year, while the lowest-paid 10 percent made about $28,000 yearly. The middle 50 percent of medical and public health social workers had annual incomes between $35,500 and $57,600.

According to the BLS, medical and public health social workers who were employed in local government made an average yearly income of around $44,000 in 2008. Those who worked in the home healthcare service industry made an average income of just under $47,000. Workers employed at hospitals or other medical facilities were paid more than medical or public health social workers in other industries, with a yearly income of more than $51,000 on average.

Mental health and substance abuse social workers made average annual incomes of around $37,000 in 2008. The highest-paid 10 percent of these workers made an average of around $61,000 per year. The median annual income of the lowest-paid 10 percent was around $21,000. The middle 50 percent made between $28,000 and $48,000 per year.

In 2008, the average yearly wages for people in industries that employ the largest numbers of mental health and substance abuse social workers were:

Outpatient care centers	$36,660
Individual and family services	$35,900
Residential mental retardation, mental health and substance abuse facilities	$33,950

[From http://www.bls.gov/oco/ocos060.htm]

Social and Human Service Assistants

Work Environment

Social and human service assistants work in a variety of conditions. Some assistants work in clinics or hospitals. Others work in offices or residential facilities. In certain cases, social and human service assistants may need to travel to see clients. Their work may be dangerous in rare instances, though employers make sure their workers are as safe as is possible. Occasionally, assistants in the social and human service field may work on weekends or at night.

As a social worker, you probably won't get rich, but you will be able to help people in need, which may fulfill you more than money.

EMPLOYMENT

In 2008, the Bureau of Labor Statistics reported that social and human service assistants held approximately 352,000 jobs, and 65 percent of these jobs were in the healthcare and social assistance industries. Around 24 percent of social and human service assistants were employed by either state or local government.

EARNINGS

The average wages for social and human service assistants in 2008 were around $27,000 per year. The highest-earning 10 percent of social and human service assistants earned just over $43,500 yearly, while the lowest-earning made yearly incomes of under $18,000. Of all these workers, the middle 50 percent earned annual incomes between $21,000 and $35,000.

Social and human service assistants who worked in state government made an average yearly income of approximately $35,500, while those working for local government earned an average of around $32,000 annually.

Did You Know?

Twenty-four percent of social workers are part of a union or in jobs that are covered by a union contract, also known as a collective bargaining agreement. A collective bargaining agreement allows workers to discuss the terms of their employment—including pay, benefits, and hours—as a group rather than as individuals.

Those working in family services made yearly incomes of around $26,000. Social and human service assistants working in substance abuse facilities made an average annual income of just $23,500, according to the Bureau of Labor Statistics.

CAREERS IN SOCIAL WORK: MEDICAL AND PUBLIC HEALTH SOCIAL WORKERS

Medical and public health social workers are responsible for:

- advocating for their clients or patients in times of hardship. This means taking the interests of the client into consideration and arguing the position of the client in any disagreements.

- working with other professionals (including medical personnel such as doctors and nurses) in order to get clients the treatment and care they need.

- recommending organizations or resources within the community designed to help clients in recovery from an illness. These resources may include legal help, financial assistance, housing programs, or job search assistance.

- helping clients adjust to daily life while recovering from illness.

- coordinating *physical therapy* or other forms of care during recovery.

- planning the way in which clients will move from one program or medical facility to another.

- speaking with family members of individuals who have medical illnesses about how they can support and can cope with the emotional hardship of a sick loved one.

- observing changes in the client's status or well-being and altering treatment plans accordingly.

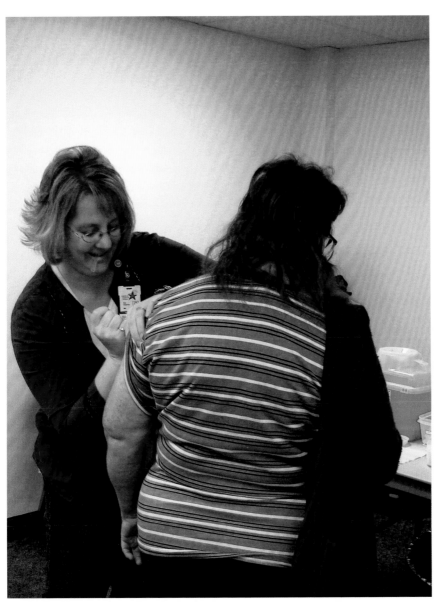

Public health workers, like this one working at a vaccine clinic, aim to prevent disease and promote health at the population level. Public health social workers work to reach these goals by focusing on the psychological and social factors that impact health.

- keeping clients on track with their treatment plans, recording progress toward treatment goals, and reporting progress to supervisors (if needed).

- understanding problems that may keep clients from getting the proper treatment or care, and coming up with solutions to alleviate any problems that arise.

SKILLS AND EXPERIENCE

In addition to skills that are directly applicable to their daily work, many medical and public health social workers will need to demonstrate knowledge outside their field. A solid understanding of medicine can help social workers understand the treatment plans their clients must follow. Social workers with this knowledge can more accurately assess the needs of their clients, as well as better work with doctors to plan treatment. Medical and public health social workers can also benefit from knowledge of psychology and therapy.

In cases involving terminal illness, medical and public health social workers may need to understand differing cultural perceptions of disease, death, and grieving. Sensitivity to different interpretations of what it means to die can serve social workers well. Knowledge of the history of different ethnicities and cultures can allow social workers to better connect with clients and their families.

If You Have a Creative Personality . . .

You might enjoy combining your artistic tendencies with a career in social work. Music and art can be useful tools when working with people who need help—but keep in mind that the focus of social work is always meeting people where they are in their real lives and helping them find solutions to the problems they face. Your ability to think in original ways may be particularly useful, however, since it will allow you to think "outside the box," finding fresh new approaches to ongoing problems in people's lives.

If You Have a Realistic Personality . . .

You may find that the problems a social worker encounters are too "messy" for your taste. You probably prefer to work with situations where the solutions will be something you can see and touch, where you can use practical tools and mechanical know-how to build a better world.

No one is useless in the world who lightens the burden of another.

—Charles Dickens

ABOUT THE QUOTE

As a social worker, it's unlikely you will ever be a millionaire. You should be able to earn enough to support yourself comfortably—but you won't be rich. So this isn't the field for you if money is your primary goal! If, instead, your goals are to make a difference in others' lives, then this could be the right path for you to follow.

CHAPTER 4
JOB OUTLOOK

Words to Know

baby boomers: People born during a period of high birthrates, especially those born in the United States after World War II, between 1946 and 1965.

integrating: Combining different things or groups so they make a whole that works well.

privatizing: Moving from government control to private ownership.

Over the next decade, the demand for social workers and assistants in social and human services is expected to grow faster than the average for employment growth across all other industries and occupations. With a population that is getting older as the *baby boomer* generation ages, workers who understand the care and services that senior citizens and their families need will find themselves most qualified to find work. Though the economic crisis of 2008 is still affecting many states around the country, meaning less money for some social programs, employment is on track to rise in almost every area of social service. Both social workers and social and human services assistants have good chances for finding work in their field.

Social Workers

The Bureau of Labor Statistics (BLS) projects that employment of social workers is going to grow faster than the average rate of growth across all industries over the next few years. While the average rate of growth in employment is expected to be around 11 percent by 2018, employment of social workers is expected to grow by 16 percent.

The BLS expects job prospects to be good for those seeking positions in social work. The number of workers seeking jobs will be roughly equal to the number of jobs available over the next few years—which is good news! Social workers are projected to be in higher demand in rural areas as well.

Employment Changes in Specific Social Work Fields

Social workers specializing in the care of senior citizens (gerontological social workers) will see the most new opportunities for work. As the population as a whole ages, both health care and social services workers will be in high demand. More and more private social services agencies will also be hiring social workers as demand increases.

Employment of child, family, and school social workers is projected to grow by about 12 percent. These workers will be needed to look into child abuse cases, find foster homes for children who

Social workers who work with the elderly are projected to have excellent job prospects due to increases in the country's older population.

Employment Projections for Social Workers through 2018		
Job Category	Projected Employment, 2018	Percent Change from 2008
Total	745,400	16
Child, family, and school social workers	328,700	12
Medical and public health social workers	169,800	22
Mental health and substance abuse workers	164,100	20
Social workers, all other	82,800	13

Overall job prospects are projected to be good for social workers. Mental health and substance abuse social workers are expected to enjoy the largest employment growth.

have been neglected, and coordinate child adoptions. State and local governments hit hard by budget crises will have a harder time employing new child, family, and school social workers. Government is traditionally the employer of the largest number of these workers. While some funding constraints may hold back some employment growth, schools are upping their enrollments and need more school social workers to cope with larger student populations. The additional influence of new policies about *integrating* children with disabilities into schools with kids who are not disabled will call for more school social workers to be hired in schools. The balance between the need for new social workers and the financial concerns of governments will determine the actual growth of employment for child, family, and school social workers.

Employment for mental health and substance abuse social workers is on track to grow around 20 percent through 2018, according to the BLS. This rate of growth is almost double that of the average occupation. Workers who specialize in substance abuse social work will be in particularly high demand. As societal attitudes toward drug abuse and addiction change from a more law-enforcement centered view to one of treatment and care, new social workers will be needed to assist individuals entering rehabilitation programs. While many drug abusers are being sent to treatment rather than prison, those who are sent to prison are also being required to attend drug abuse treatment. Some private employers may seek to hire substance abuse social workers over more costly psychologists.

New legislation also mandates that many insurance programs cover individuals for mental health treatment as they would cover treatment for physical ailments. This may open the door for new opportunities for employment in mental health social work.

Growth in the employment of medical and public health social workers is on track to be around 22 percent through 2018, double that of the average occupation. These social workers will be in high demand because of the growing needs for social services and medical care among the elderly. They will also be needed to consult with families dealing with an aging relative. Job opportunities for medical social workers who have experience with senior citizens' care will be numerous over the next few years. The number of facilities dedicated to caring for the elderly is on the rise as well, allowing more social workers to find employment in nursing homes and home care agencies.

JOB PROSPECTS

The Bureau of Labor Statistics expects job prospects to be good for those seeking employment in social work. As many older social workers retire, they will need to be replaced with new social workers. In addition, growth in the overall need for social workers will allow many more people to enter this field. Due in part to this growth, as well as the talent of workers in the job market, those looking for employment should expect qualified competition. More social workers will be competing for a smaller number of positions in urban and suburban areas, where there are more social work training programs. Workers will find much

Real-Life Career: Tina Levin
Medical Social Worker, HIV Counseling Coordinator

Tina Levin didn't know she wanted to be a social worker until she realized her need to help people, after already pursuing two successful careers. At forty, Tina left her job as a high school teacher and started her new life as a social worker by going back to school.

In college, Tina had studied biology at the advice of her parents. She didn't much care for the field, but she knew it would come with good job opportunities after graduation. "I thought I could work as a lab technician, never knowing how important it was to like your work," she says.

After graduation she worked at the National Institutes of Health as a researcher. Tina didn't enjoy the work, however, and ended up leaving to pursue teaching a foreign language at the high school level. Tina still felt that she needed to do more to help people, though, and left her job to get her BSW and then MSW.

Today, Tina works as a social worker and an HIV counselor at the National Institutes of Health. She speaks with patients who have HIV or AIDS about how their disease affects them, as well as with their families. Tina works with doctors, patients, and families, to make sure that those with HIV and AIDS get the care they need. She also works at a clinic for the uninsured two days a week. Tina's passion for her work, she says, comes from making connections with her patients. "I chose to become a social worker and an HIV counselor because I can play a role in helping people become themselves," Tina says.

(From http://science.education.nih.gov/LifeWorks.nsf/Interviews/ Tina+Levin.)

less competition and much higher demand for social workers in rural areas.

Social workers specializing in senior citizen care and services will be in particularly high demand in the next decade. In addition, substance abuse social workers will also find more job opportunities.

SOCIAL AND HUMAN SERVICES ASSISTANTS

Employment of social and human services assistants is expected to grow much faster than the average for all other jobs, according to the BLS—by almost 23 percent through 2018. Fewer workers will be competing for a wide range of job opportunities in many different fields of social and human services assistance. Workers with more than a high school education will be particularly well qualified for these positions.

Did You Know?
In 2008, the Bureau of Labor Statistics reported that 139,000 people were working as medical and public health social workers. Through 2018, that number was projected to grow by almost 66,000.

EMPLOYMENT CHANGES

As is the case with the growth in employment among social workers, the aging American population's need for care and services will drive much of the employment growth for social and human services assistants. The social service sectors that elderly citizens require help from most are meal delivery, in-home care, and

Child, family, and school social workers are projected to have slower job growth than the other types of social workers. However, special education laws will increase demand for social workers in schools.

medical support. Jobs opportunities will be particularly numerous for assistants seeking work in these areas. In addition, mental health and substance abuse are two specializations of social work that the BLS reports will require many new assistants over the next few years.

Job opportunities at private social service agencies are projected to increase in number, as well. As budget problems at the state and local level become more serious, many government agencies contract private service agencies to save money, *privatizing* the administration of some social services.

Despite budget cuts, the number of social and human services assistants employed by state and local government will grow, according to the BLS, though not quite as fast as in other sectors of assistance. The level of funding available to governments is often the determining factor in employment growth for social and human services assistants.

JOB PROSPECTS

According to the BLS, job prospects for social and human services assistants are projected to be very good. More opportunities will be open to workers who have more than a high school education. Workers who are retiring or move to other positions will need to be replaced by new employees. Workers looking for social and human service assistant jobs will find more competition for a small number of positions in urban areas. As is the case in social work, fewer social and human service assistants will be competing for jobs in rural areas.

If You Have an Investigative Personality . . .

You may enjoy putting your skills to work to find practical answers to families' and individuals' problems. Chances are, however, you'd prefer a career where you would have more opportunities to use math and science than you would in social work.

If You Have an Enterprising Personality . . .

You might enjoy a management position in social work. In a job like this you would have plenty of chances to let your energetic, sociable, and ambitious nature shine, and your abilities to be a leader would make you effective both with clients and staff. Remember, though, that social work, as with almost any career field, requires that you begin at an entry level. Your dedication and good work at lower-level jobs are what allow you to be promoted to management-level positions.

FURTHER READING

Cohn, Jessica. *Top Careers in Two Years: Education and Social Services*. New York: Ferguson, 2008.

Garner, Geraldine. *Careers in Social and Rehabilitative Services*. New York: McGraw-Hill, 2008.

Lambert, Stephen. *Great Jobs for Sociology Majors*. New York: McGraw-Hill, 2008.

Marek, Rosanne. *Opportunities in Social Science Careers*. New York: McGraw-Hill, 2004.

Paradis, Adrian. *Careers for Caring People and Other Sensitive Types*. New York: McGraw-Hill, 2003.

FIND OUT MORE ON THE INTERNET

American Council for School Social Work
www.acssw.org

Council on Social Work Education (CSWE)
www.cswe.org

International Federation of Social Workers (IFSW)
www.ifsw.org

The Mental Health Social Worker
www.mhsw.org

National Association of Black Social Workers
www.nabsw.org

National Association of Social Workers
www.socialworkers.org

National Association of Social Workers, Social Work Career Center
careers.socialworkers.org

School Social Work Association of America
www.sswaa.org

DISCLAIMER

The websites listed on this page were active at the time of publication. The publisher is not responsible for websites that have changed their address or discontinued operation since the date of publication. The publisher will review and update the websites upon each reprint.

BIBLIOGRAPHY

Onetcenter.org, "Child, Family, and School Social Workers," http://online.onetcenter.org/link/summary/21-1021.00 (1 April 2010).

Onetcenter.org, "Medical and Public Health Social Workers," http://online.onetcenter.org/link/summary/21-1022.00 (1 April 2010).

Onetcenter.org, "Mental Health and Substance Abuse Social Workers," http://online.onetcenter.org/link/summary/21-1023.00 (1 April 2010).

Onetcenter.org, "Social and Human Service Assistants," http://online.onetcenter.org/link/summary/21-1093.00 (1 April 2010).

United States Department of Labor, Bureau of Labor Statistics, "Social and Human Service Assistants," http://www.bls.gov/oco/ocos059.htm (29 March 2010).

United States Department of Labor, Bureau of Labor Statistics, "Social Workers," http://www.bls.gov/oco/ocos060.htm (29 March 2010).

INDEX

PICTURE CREDITS

Creative Commons Attribution 2.0 Generic
    Sterling Communications: pg. 18
    vic15: pg. 24

Fotolia.com
    Alexander Raths: pg. 30
    Bethany Brawn: pg. 48
    Carly Hennigan: pg. 8
    Destonian: pg. 33
    Sandor Kacso: pg. 51
    Xavier MARCHANT: pg. 24
    Yuri Arcurs: pg. 36

United States Air Forces
    Michael B. Keller: pg. 12

United States Army
    Bill Mossman: pg. 11

To the best knowledge of the publisher, all images not specifically credited are in the public domain. If any image has been inadvertently uncredited, please notify Harding House Publishing Service, 220 Front Street, Vestal, New York 13850, so that credit can be given in future printings.

ABOUT THE AUTHOR

Camden Flath is a writer living and working in Binghamton, New York. He has a degree in English and has written several books for young people. He is interested in current political, social, and economic issues and applies those interests to his writing.

ABOUT THE CONSULTANT

Michael Puglisi is the director of the Department of Labor's Workforce New York One Stop Center in Binghamton, New York. He has also held several leadership positions in the International Association of Workforce Professionals (IAWP), a non-profit educational association exclusively dedicated to workforce professionals with a rich tradition and history of contributions to workforce excellence. IAWP members receive the tools and resources they need to effectively contribute to the workforce development system daily. By providing relevant education, timely and informative communication and valuable findings of pertinent research, IAWP equips its members with knowledge, information and practical tools for success. Through its network of local and regional chapters, IAWP is preparing its members for the challenges of tomorrow.